# The Long Journey to Technical Leadership

## *Rules* and *Mistakes*

## L.S. Bozhinov

# Dedication

To my family and friends, for their love and support.

To my colleagues over the years, one and all, for making my professional path so interesting and helping me gain the insights contained in this book.

To my beloved partner, Kristina, without whom life would be devoid of meaning and whose unwavering love makes every day better than the previous one.

And finally, to you, the reader - for joining me on this journey.

# Table of Contents

# Chapter 0: A few words before we begin…

If I've done my job correctly, this book will be of some use to people across the experience spectrum in the world of Software Engineering. And that's a big *if*, of course, but I do hope that each and every one who is reading this will glean some value from my thoughts, and opinions, and insights.

The first few chapters will deal with the broader context of our industry (from my perspective) and attempt to provide a high-level overview of some of the most pertinent issues. The guidance contained therein should be especially helpful to people who are only now starting out and are wondering which path to take.

We will then transition to a quick overview of the skills, habits, knowledge, and understanding one should strive to build along the way to becoming a Tech Lead, Team Lead, Lead Engineer, Master of the Arcane Arts, etc. These several chapters are primarily concerned with the prerequisites to assuming a leadership role and how one should go about building themselves up for such a position.

Finally, the focus will shift to the transition period to that fundamentally new role, as well as the burden and privilege of leading a team, bearing the responsibility for a project, and defining a clearer vision for yourself and those around you.

## Disclaimer #0

The book you're about to read is nothing more and nothing less than my perspective on the industry, stemming from my subjective experience. Your mileage may vary, especially if you decide to treat it as a recipe book for success.

## Disclaimer #1

This is *not* a coding tutorial. We will not focus on code, but rather the context, the *other* half of the equation – the oft-underutilised soft skills and the less-than-quantifiable interpersonal aspects of the Software Engineering world.

## Disclaimer #2

I use the titles Tech Lead and Team Lead sort of interchangeably throughout the book (though that's not really accurate). What I mean by either is a person who divides their time roughly equally between writing code and managing a team.

## Ready, set, go...

So, all of that now said and done, we can start. And, as with most worthwhile things, the journey will be long and hard... but let us begin nonetheless.

# Chapter 1: A Map to Betterland

## In Lieu of an Introduction

Being a representative of that fidgety, anxious, neurotic generation which many people simply dub Millennials is becoming an odd mixture of an honour mark and social stigma.

In industries like IT, especially in the context of popular outsourcing destinations, we software engineers are the perfect example of the best – but also the worst – that our generation has to offer.

This early chapter will refer to the specific context of outsourcing with all of its gory and glorious details. And believe me when I tell you, it's not all smiles and rainbows out here. Or should I say it's not avocado toast and pumpkin Frappuccinos (if that's even a thing). Either way, you'll have to forgive me any negative opinions and mild disillusionment that may follow.

But I digress. Let's start by saying that in many an outsourcing destination, the sizable gap between living standards and earning potential has made our particular group entitled and dismissive of certain aspects of reality (more on that later).

Admittedly, the main reason for this stems from the fact that even semi-competent software engineers are a hot market commodity. They only need to do the bare minimum to keep their respective client happy and to stay billable (Time & Materials, preferably).

This in turn means that the companies employing said engineers are raking in huge amounts with insane profit margins. The outsourcing company is obviously very happy to be able to do that. The client is happy to pay less than they would in their own countries for (relatively) good engineers. The developer is also quite happy to get paid quite handsomely for work that is just good enough to preserve the status quo.

And therein lies the gist of the problem: the lack of quality. Because *quality* is but another word for *value*. And that's what each and every client is actually paying for. To my great surprise, for the time being, this untenable situation is somehow ticking along quite well. But I'm a firm believer that it is unsustainable – and that it should be *unacceptable*. For example, every single day, companies hire the wrong people and hope for the best. From my vantage point, it looks like a very sink-or-swim process – and it really should be more robust.

Yet, to be fair, recruitment is far from the only variable in this equation. The lack of foresight and strategic planning for the long-term, the over-eagerness to attain short-term profits, and the lumbering, bureaucratic top-down approach to leadership all contribute to a model that everyone in our industry ought to dub obsolete at best and broken at worst. At the very least, they really should be amazed that said model actually generates some impressive bottom lines here and there.

Perhaps the worst thing is, the situation portrayed above often leads to lazy devs who cannot be bothered to learn anything new, ask for pay raises every other month, and deliver no real value (other than monetary) to their companies. Only to jump ship at the first opportunity to put into practice that ever-present idea of more money for less work. Add to that the influx of new hires who are only drawn to the industry by the high salaries, and it suddenly becomes quite hard to find Amazing Software Engineers.

It is, of course, not all bleak. There is hope for all who choose to seek it. It is far from impossible to find the above-mentioned good engineers. There are more than a few out there. After all, being better than average is not difficult. One must only do more than the bare minimum to achieve that in the context delineated above. Being great on a larger scale, however, requires more – a lot more. Why is that the case, you may wonder?

First, because keeping your technical skills current and constantly striving to update them can only ever happen, if you truly *love* programming. Loving the thrill of climbing the career ladder will not be enough. Chasing the next pay raise will not be enough. Rather, you must feel an inexorable need to explore this infinite realm at all times. It is, undoubtedly, a field which will demand a lot of your intellectual prowess, time, and energy. Being an amazing software engineer is far from easy, trust me – I know a couple of those, and it takes a lot of blood, sweat, and tears.

Second, because you must bring quality and professionalism to everything you do and demand it of others. And that takes more than one might think. Raising the bar for yourself requires will and fortitude, and grit, and perseverance. Helping others raise themselves to a higher standard is much more difficult. You must *inspire* and *be inspired*. *Be* better to *make* others better.

Our greatness is then only determined by the boldness of the steps we take towards it. We are an industry of lofty goals and grand words. Of dreamers who often forget to walk their talk.

At the same time, however, we all know that Software Engineering is as practical a field as is possible. And, objectively speaking, all efforts to improve yourself every day will help others. Initially, the bottom line of your employer will benefit from your drive towards self-development. Then perhaps some of your colleagues, seeing your new fervour, will be inspired to rise above what they are and become what they could be.

Then the IT industry in your country will benefit, once your company begins to deliver better, higher-quality products and its competitors are galvanised to do the same. And then, maybe, finally, the scale becomes much grander. So... let's be practical, shall we?

# Chapter 2: Primary Expertise and Software Engineering

## A Tale of Two Journeys

One of the fundamental truths of Software Engineering is that the more you develop your technical skills, the easier it becomes to shift to a new pattern, paradigm, style, or language.

And yet, for someone who is at the very beginning of the long journey to Senior Engineer (more on that in Chapter 13), the question of whether or not you should specialise in one tech stack or try to become a jack-of-all-trades is quite pertinent – as well it should be, for time and effort are the main currency you have to get there. Allow me to convince you that it's not a great idea to waste them.

## Disclaimer: Whatever Works for You

If trying to become a full-stack engineer and a data scientist, and a Machine Learning guru at the same time is something you can do with any measure of success, go for it. While you're at it, why not also develop some Computer Vision and Natural Language Processing expertise? If it still doesn't sound quite enough, you could always spend some time on your blockchain skills.

The point I'm trying to make with the *reductio ad absurdum* argument above is that an attempt to become great at too many aspects of being a Software Engineer at the same time will – at best – lead to being passable at some and terrible at others. There are, of course, some *wunderkind* exceptions to this rule: if you're one of them, please feel free to ignore this particular piece of advice.

While I would never *discourage* anyone from pursuing their curiosity (on many an occasion, in fact, I have done the exact opposite), I do believe that one tends to dig deeper, if they start off with the intent to specialise in a certain skill set.

It is much more likely that you will become an expert, if you do that. A Master of the Craft. Or at the very least, you will become *good* at *something*. Hopefully, I don't have to convince you just how valuable that is.

## Focus!

My position on why setting your mind on one thing (at least initially) is a good approach is quite simple, and it's based on the following observation: spending time on one thing only will make you better at it *faster* (true for just about anything in life).

But there is another, even more practical, aspect to this: if you really are committed to a quick rise up the career ladder, becoming extremely good at that one marketable skill – and quickly – is a great way to do that. Especially in larger companies where your role, by its very definition, might be much more specialised than at a start-up.

The counterargument here is that smaller companies will require you to wear many hats, exposing you to lots of different technologies and concepts, and you will – by sheer necessity – become good at many things over time. Whether or not you can wait that long is completely up to you.

## Clarity and Motivation

Starting out, it certainly makes a lot of sense to have a clear target in mind for where you want your career to be heading and which technologies you'd like to master.

This will help you avoid the motivation dips and burnout (see Chapter 9) stemming from the overwhelming vastness of our field and the inevitable realisation that you will likely never master all of it – which is fine, at the end of the day, because you'd need several lifetimes to actually do that (again, *wunderkinds* excluded).

What you can *definitely* do is to make a choice, dig deep, and become amazing at that one language and ecosystem. You will find that the clear focus will help you keep your motivation up – and so will the constant feeling of moving forward. Progress is its own reward, and a tighter focus will help you 'level up' more quickly in all senses contained within that expression. And it then becomes a lot less difficult to pick up something new and fundamentally different.

## One Simple Truth

However odd it might sound in the context of this chapter and book, I do think one should always do what works best for them.

> *'So what I told you was true, from a certain point of view.'* [1] – Obi-Wan Kenobi

One things I'd always recommend is to listen to the great Master Kenobi. My thoughts and opinions stem from *my* experience. And yours might be quite different. So do what *you* want. Let your curiosity drive you. Or stay on target at all times. But whichever path you choose for your journey, do try to become better every day. *Put in the work.* That's the only real way to mastery.

# Chapter 3: The Quest-Reward Principle

## The Unexpected Benefits of Games for the Average Software Engineer

A lot has been written on the virtues of video games – and even more still on the terrible influence they allegedly are. Of course, I support the former point of view, as is clearly evident by the subtitle of this chapter, my current occupation, and my Steam library.

This will be decidedly unscientific (as the entirety of the book unsurprisingly is). There will be no substantiation of my claims. So, you know, fair warning. But lack of academic rigour aside, I still think the ideas laid out here should not be dismissed outright. They really *could* help you become a better Software Engineer.

To reiterate, therefore, I would like to state my support for the numerous individuals who have posited that moderate perusal of video games is actually good for you. I will *not*, however, focus on the correlation between first-person shooters and improved hand-eye coordination. People with far greater academic prowess than I have already confirmed that. Rather, I'd like to propose the idea of a *Quest-Reward Principle* as a beneficial force in the IT industry.

Anyone who has ever spent some time in a role-playing video game (RPG) will know what I mean by the words *Quest* and *Reward*. In that genre, the two are very obviously and directly related, i.e., in order to get the reward, you must finish the quest.

To get the Treasure, you must defeat the mean Goblin King. To marry the Princess, you must slay the fearsome Dragon. I think you more or less see now where I am headed with this, but I'll add one more example: to become a Great Software Engineer, you must (like in the cases described above) overcome Hard Challenges. These challenges may take any form imaginable – from *Write Better Code than the Day Before* to *Learn a New Programming Language Every Year,* to *There Is No Beer Fridge, Deal with It.*

They may be something you feel like doing, or a task you utterly abhor. They may feel like the grandest of victories, or soul-sucking, gut-wrenching defeats. Whatever the case may be, they always bring us closer to our goals. They are what we must *face,* so that we may become more than we were a couple of months or weeks, or days ago. We can't grow without them, and it's our duty to seek them out and face them whenever and wherever we can.

Don't get me wrong, I am not saying that we should all suddenly start enjoying the boring, repetitive tasks we are sometimes forced to do. Neither do I think that a terrible job could miraculously become great just by *wishing* (see Chapter 19). But this shift in perspective, this seemingly odd way of thinking about your daily grind *is* quite good, if I do say so myself.

Now bear with me and imagine the following: your favourite programming language becomes your Primary Weapon, Stack Overflow is a Magic Scroll of Infinite (but Dubious) Wisdom, and your client is the Damsel in Distress. Don't you just feel the urge to go forth and do battle with those bothersome Bugs?

After all, through a shift in attitude combined with concerted effort, a good job can become something truly special. In our industry, the path to victory is rather clear: finish the most difficult quests, get the best rewards. It's a simple truth, however hard it may be to apply it.

And here's the most interesting thing: this mode of thinking also pertains to life in general. If one can apply such high levels of gamification to work, why not to the rest of it, as well? Mind you, the unbounded rules of life are a bit more blurred than the finite context of an office. But it should, in theory, be possible.

Accept Quest?

# Chapter 4: The Habits That Make Us

## The Secret Arts

Here's one irrevocable truth about the tech industry: *good habits are paramount in Software Engineering.*

This may sound obvious, but if you stop to think about it, you realise that writing code for a living is ridden with a number of inherent, self-evident risks: burnout (see Chapter 9), loss of motivation and/or productivity (we touch on this in Chapter 16), becoming a Senior Engineer and ceasing to learn, and strive, and achieve (which, luckily, does not happen all that often, as we'll learn in Chapter 13).

The list is far from exhaustive, mind you. And there is no silver bullet that can actually address even this limited subset. But if there *were* some sort of magic pill, in this particular case, it would be the array of good habits you develop over the years – the earlier in your career, the better. They are a prerequisite for your long-term success, if you will. Because these are mental and behavioural models which ensure that there even *is* a 'long-term'.

*'Simplicity is the ultimate sophistication.'*

What is your specific, actionable goal each and every day? What do you do? And more importantly, why do you do it? What is your ultimate purpose when you launch that code editor?

These are, one and all, obvious questions. And, once again, their answers are more complex that one might expect. But they don't *have* to be. The truth is, we usually make things more complicated that they need to be.

Seeking to simplify in all senses of the word could be a keystone habit for you, in the sense that it will, time and again, lead you to create better code and become a better team member, engineer, and (perhaps) person (see Chapter 10 for more on the subject).

Code is but the end result of the real work of a Software Engineer – which is, believe it or not, *thinking* – and decluttering your mind, tackling the inevitable complexity of your job, finding a way to break all of it down to the smallest, simplest, easiest-to-understand-and-reason-about chunks will make your life *a lot* better. Chapter 8 discusses how to deal with complexity in more detail, but suffice it to say, striving for simplicity always pays off in the end.

> 'The greatest glory in living lies not in
> never falling, but in rising every time
> we fall.' – Ralph Waldo Emerson

In my experience, there are three lessons one ought to learn early on when it comes to failure.

The first is that *it's inevitable* and you must cultivate both a lack of an ego and a fair bit of endurance. You end up learning this eventually, if you last long enough.

The second is that it's a lot easier to pick yourself up and try again when you're not doing it by yourself. Having a great team makes it all so much easier.

The third is that you should always try to get there as early as possible: hit the bottom quickly, so that you might start the long road towards success without spending too much time in the metaphorical woods. For example, it is common knowledge that a start-up must get to an MVP as soon as possible, because they either fail fast, pivot, and try again – or they reach the end of the line. Which most of the time, they do.

These observations hold true both at the macro scale of a large company and at the micro level of writing code. You would be wise, therefore, to sit down and think about the problem for a bit, create your mental models, and then get on with typing on that keyboard – because the sooner you fail, the better.

*'Fear is the path to the dark side.'* [2] –
*Yoda*

The little green Master Jedi is, as always, right: being afraid *can* lead you down a path you really ought not to take. But even worse, it could keep you frozen in analysis paralysis, it could keep you from making mistakes – and therefore growing. Because the best habit to cultivate is to always be a student. Always be willing to change, learn, grow, and evolve. Seek feedback constantly, and you can avoid most of the unpleasant emotions you might otherwise encounter.

There is no better illustration of this than the near-inevitable clash with stress and anger. After all, we work with people and deadlines – two things that always lead to at least *some* levels of those negative emotions. In the Software Engineering world, this might also cause apathy and burnout – which, although not as momentous as falling to the dark side and becoming a Sith Lord, is still to be avoided if possible.

And trying to be in complete control, to enforce your will onto a codebase, colleague, team, or company is almost always a losing battle and a poignant example of a whirlwind of stress, anger, and other dark-side-inducing emotions.

So learn to let go of control – of the deep-seated desire to write all the code yourself, because no one else could possibly do it as well as you can. Not only is that mode of thinking an unofficial blocker for ever becoming a Tech Lead, for example, but it's also a delusion of the highest order. And we always know that to be the case, however much our egos and our insecurities might try to cloud our vision.

The truth is, there is much fear even in the best Engineers I've met. Nevertheless, they have learned how to master it, forgone the desire to always be right, and become the calm at the centre of the storm.

And so could you.

# Chapter 5: Humility and Software Engineering

---

## On Leaving the Code Better Than We Found It

There are quite a few well-known character archetypes when it comes to people who write code. They're so common, one could almost consider them a natural extension of the Jungian archetypes (look up Carl Jung for more details).

For example, quite often, we are the Awkward Outsider. Or the Smart Kid (you know, the one who loved maths in high school and got bullied every day). I have lost count of the number of times I've seen these two types of portrayals of brilliant software engineers, elite hackers, or wunderkind computer geniuses. And I just realised how much the two examples overlap. But I would like to draw your attention to another, more recent, character archetype: the Arrogant Asshole.

For better or worse, programming has become relatively cool due to the incredible demand for this skill at this point in time... and probably the foreseeable future. From a certain point of view, we *do* possess knowledge and we *can* solve problems that are largely unfathomable to the majority of people outside of our industry. But the same holds true for just about any complex domain – and is definitely not valid justification for rampant elitism and arrogance.

> 'His abilities have made him, well,
> arrogant.' [3] – Obi-Wan Kenobi

Master Kenobi's observation regarding his Padawan's growing prowess with the Force and the arrogance caused by that is a fascinating analogy to what we can see all around us. Of course, all of this has been written before, and it will (most likely) be written again. It can safely be classified as the proverbial 'old news'. We've cast similar light on just about any human endeavour or aspect of human knowledge, which is only to be expected: after all, arrogance is not exclusive to our industry. But since this book is (more or less) about Software Engineering, this is what I *should* focus on.

And Obi-Wan is, as usual, correct... and by that I mean that code and humility rarely go together these days. Especially when one takes into account the fact that in some countries, this increased demand has led to rather good remuneration for IT jobs. Which has only served to compound the above-mentioned arrogance.

But what the Arrogant Asshole forgets is that knowledge and/or money should not exempt us from being a Decent Human Being (yet another archetype we should petition to add to Jung's list). And the two modes of behaviour are sort of mutually exclusive.

Personally, I've always dreaded being part of the first group. To me, seeking a more humble perspective is its own reward, though I have failed to achieve it on far too many occasions. Nevertheless, humility is a fascinating thing in the context of the tech industry. When you turn off your ego for a second, you can realise how little you actually know, you can begin to care about the thoughts and opinions of people in your team, you can try to do good work and leave the code a little better than you found it.

At the end of the day, what we are doing is still a job, a.k.a., something that allows us to make a living that is not, in and of itself, somehow better or nobler than any other way of earning said living. If we were doing neurosurgery, the conversation would be a bit different. But as it stands, the world can go on without the individual struggles of most of us. After all, we all show up at the office (or sit down on our couches) to write code and build stuff. Sometimes, if we're lucky, that stuff is even cool.

Don't get me wrong, I have absolutely no desire to diminish the value of a great, fulfilling day of work – let alone the value our industry adds to our global society. Each and every one of us should take pride in our craft and enjoy the long road to a mastery that we may or may not attain. Though your mileage may vary depending on your definition of mastery.

There are those select few – more like several thousand, really – out of the circa 26 million developers alive at the time of writing in the world who work on ground-breaking, paradigm-shifting technologies. Fewer still are the people who have actually changed the world and truly made it a better place.

And I'm not saying that we shouldn't want to be like them or follow their example, or strive to attain the same heights. On the contrary – one should always strive to achieve as much as possible, go as far as possible, and become the best version of themselves. But correlation does not equal causation, at least in this case.

My point is, it's not okay to be the Arrogant Asshole. And it shouldn't be. So choose your archetype wisely.

# Chapter 6: Refactoring

## Initial Targets, Preserving Existing Functionality, and the Challenges of Clean Code

Writing code, it has often been said, is both challenging and rewarding at the same time. The same is especially true when the time comes for a quick round of refactoring. The experience can range from *Smooth Sailing and Clear Skies* to *The Perfect Storm Awaits Us Brave Poor Souls.* So how do we make sure it's the former, rather than the latter?

## Define 'Clean'

There are so many aspects to what makes code clean that it warrants its own separate discussion. Also, so much has already been written on the subject that I'm assuming some basic familiarity with the concept for the purposes of this chapter. If that is not the case, the Internet is a treasure trove of information about the fundamental principles of Software Engineering, best practices for the current language you are using, why refactoring is important, etc. There are also *a few* good books out there: I encourage you to spend some time reading through them. Think of it as an investment, because it *will* pay off down the line.

## Initial Targets: the Worst Code or the Code that Changes Most Often, or Both?

Starting a major refactoring of your codebase is always challenging – at the very least because you have to decide *where* to start. If you're anything like me, there are infinitely more questions in your mind than answers. Do you target the very worst mess you can find and try to untangle it as you slowly descend into madness? Or do you go for the code that is changing on a daily basis – the one with the constantly evolving functionality which is the *de facto* backbone of the product?

For better or worse, one does not exclude the other. And yet, whether or not they are discrete entities, I would argue that one should start with the latter. Not only will you ensure that the rest of your application has a strong foundation, but you will also develop a deeper understanding of its Core and be better able to build on top of it in the future.

## Not All Code was Created Equal: Some Is Better and Will Always Be

I think the opinion I shared above stems from my ideas on the broader question of which code should be the cleanest. When it comes to choosing what to target first during a major refactoring, it bears repeating that it should be the code you'd call the backbone of your product, the fundamental logic – the Core, if you will. It *must* be the first to become pristine.

If it already is, move on to the next piece that needs attention. If that is not the case, I'd always start there. Then follow through in descending order of importance. Randomness can be fun from time to time, but not when it comes to a major overhaul of your codebase. Ideally, you have created a thorough plan, accounted for contingencies, and made certain that there are as few unpleasant surprises in the entire process as possible.

## Tests and Refactoring, or How *Not* to Break Everything.

The single most important thing when refactoring code is to preserve or extend the existing functionality – and to take extreme care not to break it. Because the work done on cleaning up the code becomes worthless, if the user can no longer access their account after our changes were deployed. And the more complex the codebase is, the greater the likelihood of that (or other) unfortunate side effects becomes. Briefly put – and I'm sure I'm saying nothing new here, not breaking stuff can be quite the challenge.

So how can we avoid that? In my experience, the best way is to have *objective proof* that the code still works after our changes. And by that I mean tests, of course. We'll discuss them in more detail in the next chapter, but suffice it to say, they are an invaluable tool when refactoring code, for the simple fact that they provide additional confirmation that functionality is preserved beyond the slow, manual, build-and-have-a-quick-look approach. Our QA team will definitely thank us for the decrease in easy-to-catch-and-quick-to-fix bugs that testing our code effects.

To put this into perspective, imagine we are refactoring a huge, complex class (if we go the OOP route, of course). How do we usually go about doing that? We break methods spanning several screens down into chunks of code that *actually do one thing*. Or we split the code across several new files. Or – most likely – both.

And herein lies the problem: unless that code is covered by tests, we *cannot* be certain that it works exactly as it did before our changes. If it is properly tested, we need but adjust and redistribute them to reflect the new state of the codebase. If there are no tests, then that is where we should *begin*. However difficult or unpleasant it may be to add tests where none existed previously, that is the best way to ensure we don't break something, somewhere, somehow.

At the end of the day, perhaps the greatest challenge when refactoring terrible code is not purely technical. Rather, it is to get the buy-in to ever *reach* that state where code could be considered clean. This process requires a lot of time and effort – an upfront cost that not everyone is willing to pay.

But getting to the state described above is always worth it in the end, because the result of that effort is code which is easier to maintain, extend, change, and reason about: i.e., *Clean Code.* And while it *is* loads of work, it's always fun and fulfilling, making something *objectively better* than it was before.

As you grow in your career, you will have to learn not only how and when to refactor, but how to *make* that time and get that buy-in from your Team Lead, PM, Scrum Master, etc. Eventually, you will be the one who decides what the priority of refactoring tickets should be. When that happens, remember why we refactor and try to encourage your team to do it as often and as thoroughly as they can.

At the end of the day, we aim to create value with our efforts – and clean code will always do that much better than an absolute mess of entropy and madness.

# Chapter 7: Testing the Untested

## The More, the Better

It's often the case that a large codebase can remain more or less untested. Perhaps you moved too fast, churning out loads of new features every sprint. Or there was never much interest in writing tests to begin with. Or perhaps the project was simply inherited from another team, and now you have to make the code a bit more civilised (a.k.a., the *Legacy Code Nightmare* we all utterly dread).

Whatever the case may be, some interesting questions arise. Where do you even *begin* adding tests? How do you deal with this enormous task? And what if the code is so messy that it's practically impossible to test (spoiler alert, there is no such thing)?

## Disclaimer: Large and Complex Only!

One could argue that rewriting the code completely is one way to go about testing it – during refactoring, you can simplify and improve classes and make them infinitely easier to test. Testing and refactoring do go hand in hand, as I explained in the previous chapter.

However, whereas that may be easy to do in a small project where you *can* wrap your head around all the moving parts and work on improving it with relative confidence, a large and complex codebase is something else altogether. Trying to rewrite a large, untested class from scratch is almost always guaranteed to fail miserably in such a context – especially if the code doesn't really conform to established best practices, design patterns, or common sense.

## Testing 101

So where *do* we begin? I would argue that in the case described above erring on the side of safety is preferable to the alternative. To me, that means trying to isolate the smallest possible context, i.e., as with most things in software development, I usually *start with the smallest possible unit (test)*.

Adding unit tests that cover a thousand-line long class is easier said than done, and there are many ways to go about it. One of the safest, in my opinion, is to start by adding tests for the methods which are the *easiest* to test. The small victories will help motivate you for the challenges that lie ahead. And any increase in coverage is welcome – after all, the main priority is to *not* break anything. Hopefully, after some minutes, hours, or days, you will be left with only a few multi-screen, mind-boggling behemoths.

And that's where the *fun* begins.

## Slaying the Dragon

Now comes the most interesting and precarious moment in this particular approach to testing large codebases.

The huge methods you are yet to test are usually the product of a series of unfortunate events – most of them undeliberate, none of them unexpected. Or at least, that's usually been the case in my experience. They are often doing several unrelated things, have logic branching that would make the Architect from the Matrix films furrow his brow in puzzlement, and they are probably used in a dozen classes that do something completely unrelated in an entirely different feature of your application.

You could leave this code untested... but that's not really an option, is it? Why back down from such an interesting challenge? Assuming you decide to forge ahead, the only thing you *could* do to test this with any degree of confidence is to break the method down incrementally: that is, extract a small part of the code in a separate method and test it. Then rinse and repeat until the beast has been defeated.

The important thing to keep in mind is, the *entire* functionality of the method must be preserved (however shocking and surprising this may sound). What I mean is, calls to the method from other classes may only need a couple of lines that might look unrelated. But removing them could break another feature completely. This is, of course, a nightmare scenario of tight coupling, yet it's not an uncommon one. Ideally, that will no longer be the case in your codebase with the huge methods refactored and the tests written.

## This Is Just the Beginning...

Let's say you followed the approach above to its logical conclusion and now have sufficient test coverage (whatever your definition of that may be). A reasonable ROI on time and effort is, after all, subjective, but let's assume you have added enough tests to confidently do a major refactoring of your codebase, leading to more tests and refactoring, until you're finally proud of the code you've created. What do you do when that happens?

The truth is, testing is never done. Unit tests must be adjusted with each change to the imaginary class we just cleaned up and covered with tests. But it's just the first step in the process. Beyond fixing the code at the smallest unit level, one should also strive to ensure that those units work well *together*, i.e., the next logical thing to do is write integration tests.

And that should be much easier to do now that the codebase has been tested from the ground up – and at least partially refactored. Getting to this point opens up the possibility of making huge code changes with confidence and is a great step in the right direction.

But there is *always* something more you can change and extend, and improve. So go for it!

# Chapter 8: Dealing with Complexity

## Mental Models in Software Engineering

Most teams working on a project which grows to size Medium and beyond (as always, your definition may vary) will inevitably face one infamous problem: the complexity of the code increases to the point that even experienced engineers have trouble reasoning about the various moving parts. But why, one might wonder, is that such a big deal?

## The Problem

Hitting a certain level of complexity makes developing new features exponentially more difficult and increases the likelihood of new code being riddled with bugs for reasons too self-evident to get into. This in turn diminishes the overall output of the team, because a task you could previously finish in a week now requires a month to complete.

In extreme cases, progress could just about grind to a halt as the risk of new code breaking multiple features increases and people begin realising just how costly their earlier poor decisions could be.

Briefly put, you should do your best to reign in complexity as early as possible: because you either *master* it, or you *serve* it.

# How to Fix Bugs and Simplify Projects

Fortunately, there are more than a few approaches to tackling this issue. For example, and I think that's probably the best one for its simplicity, you could plan on how you will scale your code *before* you actually do it. Accounting for the growth of complexity should be an integral part in the architectural stages of your solution. Of course, quite often that's not the case (or else I would not be writing this), and you're left with pile upon pile of messy, mind-boggling, and over-engineered code that you regret ever having written.

This is a complex problem, but its solution needn't be a complex one. Simple though it may be, it's still multifaceted and far from easy to implement, and in my opinion, the most important aspect of that solution is the *mental model* we adopt when designing systems and writing code. Ultimately, we are the ones creating the additional layer of complexity where it need not exist – and quite often, we do it because we *don't take the time to think* of a better, simpler, more elegant approach.

# Reason *Must* Enter into the Equation

As I stated above, the most reasonable thing one can do is to *not* let projects become complex and over-engineered in the first place. Changing architecture two years into a project is possible – but in the vast majority of cases, that basically means we're starting from scratch. And that's not what we're discussing here. Let's assume that ship has sailed long ago. What can we do to fix the problem *after* the fact?

The solution, as I said above, is both simple and complex, but one part of it – the most important part – is *really* simple: the shift in perspective. It's all about perspective. It's all about bringing reason and order to chaos. When we add new code, we *must* ensure it's as simple as possible while still being functional. We do the same when we refactor old code.

Simpler approaches are much more likely to be correct than complex ones – and to remain correct where multiple layers of abstraction and elegant hierarchies of classes might not even compile.

What I mean to say is, this mental shift pays off in the long run.

## On the Virtues of Incremental Improvements

Keeping new code simple is far from a revolutionary idea. But it works flawlessly, and that remains the case when we apply it to *the rest* of our project. Software, by its very nature, is infinitely malleable, never quite finished. Which means it's possible to continually and perpetually improve it or screw it up – and that's what I would advocate here (improving it *ad infinitum*, I mean).

Imagine you're adding a new feature to a complex class which is part of a tangled web of dependencies and weird inheritance. Your new code is clean and simple. Therefore, you have *not* done the codebase, yourself, or your colleagues a disservice. You could leave it as it is and move on to the next feature or bug, or framework-of-the-day experiment. Or you could refactor just one method. Simplify the class just a tiny bit. Leave the code just a little better than you found it.

If everyone did that, the small, incremental improvements would compound over time. And the effects of that are *far greater* than you might think.

# Chapter 9: Burnout and Bugs

## Maintaining Sanity in the Face of Madness

In your career as a software engineer, you will most likely face more than a few bugs which are so difficult to track down, understand, and fix that they are nearly incomprehensible – and quite maddening to deal with.

These elusive issues will keep you up at night and make you regret your life choices. Or at least that's what happens to me every time I have to tackle one of them.

## The Creeping Burnout of Bugs Long Unsolved

I think there are few aspects of being a developer which are worse than the repeated failure to solve some tough bug, implement a feature with unclear requirements, etc. The more innocent a ticket looks at the beginning, the more frustrated and angry you become, if you can't find a good solution – or any solution, for that matter.

The truth is, *we've all been there.*

And it's the fear that you just aren't good enough that usually effects said anger. But what you forget is that one bug does *not* determine the breadth and depth of your abilities, nor your compatibility with the world of Software Engineering.

Giving in to those emotions leads to the unpleasant state of mind where you no longer care about solving the problem in the best possible way. Rather, you simply want to get rid of it and move on with your life. And when you reach this state of near-burnout, nothing you achieve seems to even *matter*. So what can be done to avoid that?

## Life Is Not One Game but Many

There are some bugs that you solve immediately: the path to the end goal takes shape in your mind before you've even started adding breakpoints. You try out your approach, and it's time to commit and push (assuming you've added tests, of course).

But what do you do, if the ideal situation I just described plays out a bit differently? For example, you have absolutely *no idea* where to begin or the direction you've chosen is *more than a bit wrong*.

In the former case, think a bit harder, reflect, experiment, and tinker for a while. A solution will present itself. If it doesn't, you could try discussing the issue with one of your colleagues. You'd be surprised how often the simple act of explaining the problem to someone else will lead you to its solution. If it doesn't happen automagically, they'll actually help you figure it out.

In the latter... One approach failed. Naturally, you should try again. But try something completely different, a.k.a., play the *Shift Your Perspective* game. More often than not, that will be enough. If you're still stuck, see the previous paragraph – you are part of a team *for a reason*. Software Engineering is not a solo game (with some notable exceptions, of course).

## The Unexpected Joys of Banging Your Head against the Wall

In the worst-case scenario, you will try and fail, and try again. But don't forget to enjoy the experience. Don't close up and get angry. Instead, *try to learn* from every single failure. Whatever happens with that bug, you will have become a better engineer because of it – but only if you keep calm and try to enjoy the work and the process, and the pain.

I guess what I'm trying to say is, not taking the situation too seriously is quite beneficial. It keeps your mind fresh and open to new thoughts, ideas, and experiences (including the learning kind). I think our industry would be a lot better, if we all laughed more and stressed out less.

## Game Over?

Like the legendary dragons when you first encounter them in *Skyrim* (the reference is valid until Todd Howard finally graces us with *The Elder Scrolls VI*), some bugs are simply beyond your current skills and abilities. So do the only logical thing you can: move on. Come back later, if said dragon still roams that particular part of the sky.

And though you can't reload, you shouldn't consider the time spent working on that bug wasted. Failure is the *greatest of mentors*. Early on in your career, you will fail countless times. It will get better as you gain more experience, but you will still fail quite often. After all, you'll be facing much tougher challenges as you level up.

My point is, I hope you are ready to accept that your secret weapon is that one incredible magical power called *Patience*. It's a spell unlike any other and can be used to deal with just about any long-running task you might face in the realm of Software Engineering – whether it be bug or feature, or change request, or chore.

Because very often the problem is not the ticket, the team, or the nature of the work. It's how we *choose to perceive it*.

## Beyond Burnout

Learning to maintain a modicum of optimism and to cast the *Patience* spell as you progress through your career will also prepare you for the much more challenging burnout-causing situation of rising conflict and communications breakdown within teams, as well with various stakeholders.

When you're the leader, you can't really afford to fall prey to burnout of any kind, even though the pressure on you will stem not only from technical, but also from interpersonal sources. So make sure to invest those skill points wisely – and definitely max out the *Patience* skill tree. If your path is anything like mine, you're going to be needing it a lot.

# Chapter 10: The (Un)expected Benefits of Minimalist Code

## Why Less is Often More in Software Engineering

Code minimalism is about the oft-underrated art of simplification. But it's more than just a change of syntax, style, or design pattern. Rather, it's something *deeper*: a fundamental shift in perspective that entails a rigid structure, a certain ruleset, and *a lot* of discipline.

The concept of minimalism emerged in the art world in the early sixties, but the ideas contained therein resonated with many other subcultures, including the domain of Software Engineering. We apply them daily when we try to create simpler, cleaner, more elegant code. And we most certainly *should*. Because when we take a moment to consider the alternative and realise that every new method could introduce a bug, a regression, or an indirection, the benefits of simplification become readily apparent.

So we should take the time to evaluate how much we need those lines of code. They might even turn out to be completely unnecessary, simply because the path of least resistance often coincides with the fewest new lines added.

## Minimalism v Readability?

One commonly mentioned negative aspect of striving for elegant code is the increased likelihood that said code will become less readable. And that is, arguably, often the case. When refactoring, if we're not careful, we could do more harm than good. We've covered this in Chapter 6 already, but it bears repeating. And yet, the question remains: how do we avoid this decrease in readability?

Stemming from my experience, a good rule of thumb is to make the code as simple as it possibly *can be made* while maintaining readability. Trying to make your code too clever for its own good will only increase the WTF count per minute – and that's not really something we want, do we?

Another well-adopted idea is to try limiting the focus of your code, i.e., make sure to remember the single responsibility principle when you refactor your classes – and this is especially true when adding *new* code. It's tempting to finish implementing your new functionality, add a couple of tests, and commit and push. But we both know that spending the extra time, making an additional effort, going the extra mile will pay off sooner or later.

Still, let us now bring the topic back to the alleged conflict between minimalism and readability. Spartan programming, for example, is the logical conclusion of striving for elegance and brevity. However, it usually produces less readable code, and it's easy to shoot yourself in the foot, if you don't know what you're doing. Of course, taken to the extreme, *any* good idea can become bad. But if you apply it with care and foresight, you'll be okay.

What I'm trying to say is, keep the established best practices in mind when creating new code: patterns, concepts, ideas, etc. I am a proponent of the notion that elegant code is actually inherently more readable, simply because there is *less of it*. And more importantly, there is *less nonsense* to deal with: fewer layers of abstraction or indirection which are only there to obscure the intent of the engineer who created them, less unused code, and fewer assumptions about the state of the app, or the origin of the Universe, or the colour of magic.

It requires more thought and planning ahead of time, as well as more time to implement. After all, it *is* more difficult to keep complexity in check, than to let it have free reign (revisit Chapter 8, if you've forgotten about that). And of course, it's more difficult to remove lines of code and minimise redundancy than to not code them up in the first place. But it's *always* worth it.

## Focus Determines Reality

My point is, code should be plain, focused, and perfectly organised. I would not add even a single line, if it cannot justify its existence – if it doesn't make the code, the product, and the user experience better.

If I could, I would throw that line away. Arguably, the best, most stable, most secure, and most elegant code is *the one you never write*.

But as you grow into a lead role, it will fall on you and your team to determine how much is too much for your project. It will no longer be just about personal preferences – rather, all of you, together, will shape and influence the broader context around you.

And *you*, as the leader, will have to drive that. *You* will have to be the one pushing forward towards clean, minimalist code. *You* will have to make the choice: do things *right* or do them *again*.

# Chapter 11: Code Maintenance

---

## On How Not to Shoot Your Future Self in the Foot

When you sit down to fix the next bug or implement the next feature, you are making lots of choices per minute. And those choices generally lead you down one of two paths, two quite divergent outcomes: a codebase which is better, easier to maintain, reason about, extend, and improve – or its polar opposite, a complex mess of sadness and entropy.

Writing maintainable code is related both to keeping minimalism in mind when you implement new things, and to your willingness to reign in complexity at every turn. I've argued that these two inter-related aspects of Software Engineering are of principal importance, if one wants to end up with great code. And code maintenance is the third part of the trinity. But given that maintenance and maintainability are among the – how should I put it – *less sexy* topics, I think they warrant a bit of attention.

What follows is my list of lessons learned about these topics over the years:

1. Creating maintainable code is a present to your future self – and believe you me, you will thank your past self for the extra time and effort. It's all about you. Well, not all of it, actually (see the next point).

2. You also do it to make other people (a.k.a., your team) *less miserable* at each and every point in time. Striving for maintainability, by its very nature, will usually result in code which is more readable and less likely to be riddled with bugs and bad practices. Which has the interesting effect of shifting the mood dial of your current team members from Sad to Happy – or at least to Content. But it also means new additions to the team will not

follow ugly/terrible patterns, simply because those patterns will not *exist* in your project.

3. The more you climb up the seniority ladder (see Chapter 13), the more you come to realise that we tend to spend more time trying to figure out code – be it ours or something your fellow Engineers wrote – than writing new one. Creating unmaintainable code, therefore, has a drastic impact on the performance of engineering teams, at the very least because it's more difficult and time-consuming to read and understand. This becomes doubly true when you take on the mantle of Tech Lead or Team Lead.

4. Less is more, as I previously noted – especially a few months from now. Be precise. Strive for minimum impact on the current class and least coupling with other classes. Write things with modularity as the driving idea – code is always easy to *add*, but it should likewise be easy to *remove*.

5. Another thing that has already been mentioned but bears repeating is the fact that keeping scalability and maintainability in mind *will* make you more likely to succeed in keeping complexity in check.

6. Always keep a consistent style throughout your codebase – or at the very least, try to do it. Keep to existing best practices and good habits.

7. Avoid clever code like the bloody plague.

8. Comments are a bit of a controversial topic – but my rule of thumb is, if the code is not absurdly easy to understand (a.k.a., self-documenting three- or four-liner methods), I'd add a comment. Even to the most readable code. And, depending on the seniority of my team, I would most probably aim for readability over code cleverness (see the point above). Basically, if a Junior Engineer can't figure out what the method does in ten to twenty seconds, then I haven't done my job well enough, and the method must be refactored (and a comment added). But to return to the original idea of this paragraph, if you think comments are idiotic or deadly, at least do some proper documentation of your classes *somewhere, somehow*. And keep it up to date.

9. When it comes to throw-away code, such as proof of concept implementations, quick spikes, or even an MVP, we usually forget about all of the 'rules' above. And in those situations, one objectively needn't worry about the long-term: sloppy code is okay. Just not when it's the foundation and future core of your product and must live on indefinitely. Learn to be able to recognise when to get stuff done quickly and when to focus on keeping code clean.

And yet, when all is said and done, perhaps the most important, fundamental skills, to me at least, are not really technical in nature. Rather, it's the ability to work as part of a team, to speak with the aim to convince, to listen with the willingness to understand, and to have opinions, but be prepared to change them. To lead, to follow, and to know when to do which.

It is our soft skills which ensure the long-term maintainability of code, not just our ability to write clean code. This is vital for a leader to understand – preferably *before* they become one.

# Chapter 12: Attachment is the Enemy

## Why We Must Learn to Let Go of Our Best Code

The road to becoming a Senior Software Engineer (see the next chapter for more on that) is paved with oh-so many good intentions – and far too large a number of hurdles. Some of them will stem from your environment: your team, your project, your company. But most will likely be related to you as an engineer or as a person (spoiler alert, it's Harsh Truth o'clock).

## Your Dearly Beloved

Among the most challenging of said obstacles, I think, is our inclination to become infatuated with the current best code we can write – or the one we have just written. Becoming attached to the results of our efforts is only natural, but it can also lead to a myriad of issues, not the least of which are unwarranted confidence, the lack of a desire to change the code in any way, and an inability to accept new – and possibly better – ideas. The question then arises, how do we prevent that?

> 'Kill your darlings, kill your darlings,
> even when it breaks your egocentric
> little scribbler's heart, kill your
> darlings.' [4] — Stephen King

The Master of Horror has many a brilliant insight when it comes to writing – and this one is certainly in my personal Top 5 because it's full of so much realism and acceptance. It's extremely applicable to our industry, too, as one must learn to let go of the code they simply adore. That's the first, most important, and most difficult step in your journey away from Attachment Town. So the next time you see a pull request which deletes some brilliant function you authored, take a deep breath and approve it – of course, only if there is good reason to delete said function, and the rest of the changes are not full of idiotic bugs. After all, there is a difference between being overly attached to your code and protecting the codebase from an influx of stupidity.

As ever, your mileage may vary – and in this case, it will do that depending on your definition of 'brilliant' and 'idiotic'. I should also add, perhaps, that the veracity of 'Kill your darlings!' increases exponentially with the cleverness of that code. The code review stage is a perfect time to ensure new additions to your codebase are as maintainable as possible. Of course, in my experience, that extremely clever code is the one people tend to be most defensive of during code reviews, with the *lovely* inter-team conflicts this entails.

## Alone Means Lost

By no means do I argue – or would ever do – that one should not take pride in their work or defend the choices made during its creation. What we do is, after all, interesting, and challenging, and hard work, and *ample* reason for feeling like we have *achieved* something.

Nevertheless, we are rarely capable of producing the most incredible idea or solution in complete intellectual vacuum. There is a *reasonable extent* to which we should be defending our code and our choices: and that limit is reached when a better way is made evident to us. This can occur in a myriad of ways, and it's true that sometimes the entire journey will take place in our own mind. But more often than not, the better way will be externally provided.

My point is, one should always be open to considering and be willing to accept ideas other than their own. As a leader, your reactions and attitudes will often set the standard for the rest of your team – so staying humble and reacting well to criticism is vital for the long-term success of your project.

Also, we should always keep in mind the transience of it all. Software, by its very nature, is ever-changing and ephemeral. The code you write today, however elegant or amazing, may need to go down the drain tomorrow. And that's okay. That's the way it should be.

Attachment is the Enemy, remember?

# Chapter 13: Seniority in the Software Engineering World

## Signposts on the Hero's Journey

Imagine you're a fresh graduate on the first day of your internship at INSERTNAMEHERE INC (if you actually are at that stage of your career, this chapter will definitely be of interest to you). At that hypothetical point in time, basically everyone working there has more experience than you. You're impressed by the junior devs and astounded by the skills of the regular/mid-level engineers.

And then there are the Senior Engineers: the godlike creatures who have a wealth of knowledge and are the true Masters of Advanced Programming Magic. Also known as, your Current Career Goal.

## Disclaimer: It's Just a Title

But perhaps I am the only one who experienced that moment in the way delineated above. Weird or not, this reminiscing raised the question in my mind, how *do* you define seniority in our industry?

Of course, the answer is never simple – not in the least because the interpretation of and the requirements for a Senior Engineer are quite different across companies, countries, and business domains. But I would argue that most who attain that particular title (empty or not) have certain qualities in common. Or if they don't, they most definitely *should*.

## Masters of the Arcane Arts

I would always start *any* list of requirements for *any* domain with *Boundless Curiosity*. And by that I mean, the best engineers I know are always learning, always up to date with the next big thing or set of best practices, always *pursuing mastery* of their craft.

From my point of view, mastery means that one must strive not only for breadth, but also depth of knowledge. After all, we live by the 'use the best tool for the job' mantra: i.e., the more we know about tool-job compatibility, the better. I strongly believe that Dex was right about the 'difference between knowledge and wisdom' [5] and it all starts with understanding that such a difference exists and becoming able to distinguish between the two.

But how does one go about attaining said wisdom? The only way I know is quite simple, really: practice, practice, and then practice more. The truth is, *you have to love programming* – or learn to, if you don't. Because you should be doing quite a lot of it, or at least enough to drive you forward in your career to a stage you love a fair bit more.

Admittedly, there is an art to Software Engineering, but it is beyond a shadow of a doubt *also a craft*. Thus, one should strive to always be *doing*: building side projects, solving random coding challenges, coding along with tutorials on an obscure language they don't really need to know (not always a great idea; look up Brainfuck to see why), going to conferences and meetups, giving talks (if that's their thing), contributing to open source projects (if they have the time and energy after they're done with the day job), or finding *some* way to give back to the community. There truly are so many ways to sharpen your tech skills. The important thing is, there is always *something more to be learned*, and one should never forget that.

Nevertheless, if I had to focus on specific tech abilities and/or superpowers, I'd start with the following:

1. A Senior Engineer is *not afraid to break stuff*, because they know they can fix it. There is a confidence that comes with extensive practice and the precise use of code. I'm obviously not advocating that you go and nuke your prod environment – quite the opposite, in fact. What I'm saying is, 'experience outranks everything' [6], if I may steal the line from Captain Rex. It's fundamental for success in battle against droid armies, and it's just as important in your

endless struggle against horrible code. Experience does not necessarily equate to years in the industry, mind you. What it does entail, however, is a quiet confidence that you *will* solve the problem.

2. *Thou shalt not be afraid to touch shitty code!* It doesn't matter who the author of that code is. If it's broken, fix it. If it's buggy, refactor it. *No code is sacred*. If you can make it better, do it!

3. The best engineers I know have *an indomitable will* when it comes to reigning in complexity. Because they know it's one of the toughest challenges of scaling a codebase, as we established in Chapter 8.

4. One should also have an inclination to write minimalist code. Because *code quality and style do matter*, and improving them makes everyone's lives easier (see Chapter 10).

This most certainly is *not* an exhaustive list of the hard skills one would need – but I'd say it's a good start.

## The Dev You'll Be

'Gar taldin ni jaonyc; gar sa buir,
ori'wadaasla. (Nobody cares who your
father was, only the father you'll be.)' [7]
– Mandalorian saying

If you haven't encountered the brilliant *Star Wars: Republic Commando* series by Karen Traviss, now is a great moment to add it to your reading list. It expands quite a bit on Mandalorian culture, and while it is nowadays considered Legends material, it's worth the time – nuggets of wisdom like the quote above abound, and they raise quite a few questions.

For example, and to bring the discussion back on topic, who do you become as a person while you grow as an engineer? My personal interpretation of the soft skills required for such a role is founded on several qualities. First and foremost in my mind is the *ability to lead others* and inspire team members to do better and be better. To be able to point out the right way. This may or may not mean you should possess an urge to *mentor* others – but it does mean you should have a desire to raise the bar for everyone and share what you know in *some* way.

A Senior Engineer, I believe, is also a person who can *take ownership* of most every aspect of the job: e.g., steer a project/feature from start to finish. Which is quite closely tied to the ability to take the initiative and set the direction in which a project should head: basically, a senior dev can *rarely* feel underutilised, because they know there is *always* something else to do. That something is usually quite the list, and they're able to identify the items on that list with ease – and then *determine the priority* of those items.

The points I've made in the two preceding paragraphs are, in my experience, usually balanced by humility (now is a great time to revisit Chapter 5). There are many aspects of and challenges to *staying humble* as you get better at just about anything. But in the context of Software Engineering, I'd argue that one should be able to own their mistakes (and admit them freely), stay open to new ideas, and always keep in mind that nothing is black and white – there are far too many nuances in our day-to-day jobs and in our industry more broadly.

Last – but definitely not least – is the ability to communicate across many different levels and navigate organisational complexity. Which is just a fancy way of saying that you should know when and what you should be saying – and to whom you should be saying it. It *sounds* simple. It most definitely *isn't*. And it only becomes harder when you become a leader.

At the end of the day, we work with *people* – and the ability to communicate your thoughts and ideas with clarity and precision is one of the most fundamental skills you need as an engineer. And it's one of the hardest.

## Attaining Mastery?

Mastering anything is a long and difficult journey – but in the case of becoming a Senior Engineer, it's one which is ultimately incredibly rewarding in all sense of the word. So steel your mind, trust in the strength of your will, and know that you *can* accomplish more than you think. This is true of just about anything. And it's most certainly true of Software Engineering.

# Chapter 14: Rising Above Doubt

## On Overcoming Impostor Syndrome

Have you ever felt like you're moving along quite nicely in your job in the morning – only to suddenly become overwhelmed by the boundless realm of Software Engineering at the end of the day? Have you ever felt like you don't really belong at your company; perhaps the interviewers just made a mistake? Or like suddenly everyone is better at writing code than you are – and at mentoring others, leading teams, and delivering quality products?

Basically, if you've ever felt like a fraud, like someone who *really* shouldn't be allowed to commit even a single line, let alone tell other people what they should work on and how they should write their code, you know what impostor syndrome means in the context of our industry. What you might not realise is, we've all been there. And, in some cases, we're still there: for many of us, those feelings are quite common. We just get better at pushing down the voices of doubt as we learn more and grow as engineers and leaders.

My point here, I guess, is that there are ways to deal with that. What follow are several tips to keep in mind, if and when impostor syndrome resurges.

## Knowledge and Wisdom

There are – and always will be – people who know more than you about something. Or even about *a lot* of different aspects of Software Engineering and Computer Science. Which both completely normal and absolutely fine. What you need to remember is, at a certain point in time, they *did not* know that.

But neither did they automagically gain said knowledge – rather, they did the work and spent the time necessary to attain it. And trust me, you could do the same. So if you feel the sudden urge to tinker with the tool, language, or concept in question, go for it.

## The (Un)expected Virtues of Academia

Not having a Computer Science degree does not automatically translate to never becoming a great Software Engineer. Of course, spending years at a university learning the fundamentals is an incredible head start compared to learning all of it on your own time while you're working and trying to get better at your day job. And it *is* quite undeniable that *you need to know it* to get ahead. But the good news is, you *can* learn it: all it takes is, as ever, lots of time and effort. There *are* no shortcuts – and no way to avoid the sweat and tears.

And you can trust me when I say that you *need* that knowledge to become a decent developer. As someone who stumbled into Software Engineering from the field of Renewable Energy, I can tell you that there have been many occasions where I've felt like I am playing an endless game of tag, in which I'll never be able to actually catch anyone. Yet, the secret is, *there is no game.* The only engineer you should be comparing yourself to *is the one you were yesterday.* Stay humble. And keep learning, growing, and improving – especially if you end up leading a team. That's when your personal example will have the greatest impact.

Our field is vast, and the knowledge contained therein is nearly boundless. We can – and should – spend our entire professional lives constantly learning. Whether or not we started with four years in academia will not be the final determining factor in establishing our compatibility with the industry. Yet, the *knowledge* gained from it – or the lack thereof – most definitely will. So keep that in mind as you take on the next challenge, and all the challenges thereafter.

## Semper Impostor

I'd like to share one more 'secret': impostor syndrome doesn't really ever go away, not completely. I said it earlier, and it's quite sadly the truth. Even if you reach the title of Senior Engineer (and beyond) and become the embodiment of all the virtues ascribed to it. Even if other people learn more from you than vice versa. Even if you prioritise tasks, manage multiple projects and teams, and create brilliantly-designed systems. It doesn't go away.

On the bright side, you *will* get better at dealing with the outward symptoms as you gain more experience.

One thing that might help is to take the time to look through some code which turned out to be elegant and minimalist or to remember a situation where your skills, knowledge, attitude, or perspective helped your entire team. Even someone who is just starting out will have solved at least *some* difficult problems – and thinking about those moments of triumph can be extremely liberating and helpful. The good thing is, as we grow in our careers, we get more of these shiny, happy moments to keep us going.

*'Look what I have risen above.'* [8] –
*Obi-Wan Kenobi*

Even in the most difficult of moments, Master Kenobi knew that he could not surrender to darkness. When faced with an old nemesis, one could understand, if he had let the past cloud his judgement and push him out of balance. Yet, he never did.

The lesson I took away from that incredible scene is how incredibly easy it is to allow doubt and despair to take over – but the best never do. And it's surprisingly difficult to maintain an objective perspective regarding our own successes and failures.

To be honest, both remain a mystery to me to this day. And perhaps that's for the better. But we most definitely *should* think about it. After all, what we ought to never do, is forget what we have *risen above*.

# Chapter 15: The Strength of Your Convictions

## Strong Opinions, Loosely Held

In the world of Software Engineering, we have a fascinating mantra: 'strong opinions, loosely held'. I'm sure by now you've encountered it on numerous occasions.

Personally, I think it's a brilliant summary of something so very fundamental to us doing our jobs well. And I'd like to share with you some pertinent conclusions I've reached over the years.

## Our Word is Our Bond

Because of the nature of what we do, when we voice our convictions, we *must* act on them. For example, it's never enough to say that something needs to be covered by more tests or that the code is beyond salvation and needs to be completely refactored.

If it's bothering you that much, start fixing it. If you say it, do it. Or, if you're the leader, delegate it to the team member who will learn the most from it while still finishing the task in a reasonable amount of time. That's even better for your team and project in the long run than wrapping up the task in half a day and moving on to something else.

## But It's Not Always the Best Way

One thing to keep in mind, however, is that when you fix a bug or create a new feature, your implementation may be far from the optimal way to do it. And, ideally, someone *will* point that out to you.

It happens to all of us, all the time – as it should. We *need* to be challenged by our peers and team members, because that is one of the best ways to grow as an Engineer. It doesn't matter how experienced we are, because even if we don't end up accepting someone's suggestion or critique, we at least spend time thinking about the validity of multiple different paths to a certain goal and perform some in-depth analysis of our own approach. Which is always a good thing to do at every level of seniority.

So, keep an open mind at all times. It's for the good of your project and your team, and for your own, too. Because there is *always* a better way to do something when it comes to code, and we've already talked about attachment and the disadvantages thereof in Chapter 12.

> '*The trouble with having an open mind, of course, is that people will insist on coming along and trying to put things in it.*' [9] — Sir Terry Pratchett

There is, of course, one small caveat to the mantra I espoused in the previous paragraphs, as Sir Terry so clearly states: when you invite people to change your mind, the end result might be far from desirable without some validation on your end. One should be careful, after all, when choosing their influences.

Still, some situations are quite clear-cut: for example, if you've started your first job as a Software Engineering Intern yesterday, it might be a good idea to let your more experienced colleagues tell you what you can do better. But while it may surprise some people, I believe the opposite can also be true.

My main rule is that I need a strong *why*. Change my mind. But don't tell me *that* something is better, tell me *why* it is better. I will defend what I know to work best for a certain problem, until I know that something else is objectively better, and then I *will* adopt that. In fact, I *want* to.

Strong opinions, loosely held...

# Chapter 16: Improving Performance

## What Makes or Breaks Engineering Teams

One of the major causes of poor software performance is the widespread lack of objective evaluation in our industry when it comes to what makes teams more coherent and increases their velocity. We often implement the latest buzzword and jump on the trend bandwagon without too much thinking about its compatibility with our current situation or the consequences it entails.

And therein lies the problem: the performance of engineering teams is the product of complex, interlinked systems consisting of best practices, habits, processes, and ideas. The balance of those ingredients will be different from one team to the next. And a lot of thinking and tinkering is required to find the best formula for your team.

Of course, you've probably already guessed it, it's actually very hard to find the right balance. But fortunately, there are *some* things we can do to avoid getting it horribly wrong.

## Some Dos and Don'ts for Managers and Tech Leads

At the top of my not-too-comprehensive list is the inclination to choke the motivation out of your team by drowning everyone in too much process, having too many meetings, and just generally being a micromanaging tyrant who is only interested in closing as many tickets as possible in as little time as possible.

As we've probably all hoped, this trend has been on the decline. And that should remain the case – unless, of course, something goes horribly wrong with our industry as a whole. There are few things Software Engineers hate more, in my experience, than someone pinging them about their progress every fifteen to twenty minutes.

The other side of this coin – and one just as unfortunate – is to give free reign to everyone. Let's take a moment to consider it, shall we? Because in my opinion, going for an absolutely *laissez faire* approach is almost equally bad of a decision, if only for the simple reason that we all need at least *some* structure to achieve *anything*. Undirected effort is just plain stupid.

As usual, one should strive for a balanced approach and simply try not to kill motivation with process. We should have meetings and status reports, but not *too many*. After all, if you've hired great engineers, you need to give them the space and the trust *to be great*.

Briefly put, your aim should be to learn the difference between good and bad processes in the context of your team. It may sound like a hard thing to do – and that's because it is.

## A Few More Words for Tech Leads

I would simply highlight four of the Laws I've discovered in my career so far:

1. Don't try to do everything yourself; you will most certainly fail.
2. Trust your team, and they will trust you.
3. Never keep the most challenging tasks for yourself – let others learn and grow.
4. When all is said and done, we are all only human: act accordingly.

That's it, the most important kernel of wisdom I've come across – these four rules. The good thing is, they're pretty self-explanatory, and applying them is not that complicated (though it's never easy). So go for it!

## As An Engineer, I...

But what can you do, if you're not a manager, Team Lead, or Tech Lead yet – or don't really want to be one? As it turns out, there are actually a lot of problems you could address.

For example, you could find out what slows *you* down the most and put in the concerted effort to fix it. Early on in your career, it may be lack of knowledge and/or experience. Addressing that one is straightforward, even if it isn't *always* easy.

Of course, the blockers evolve as we progress in our careers. As a Mid-level Engineer, it may be the process your team is using (see above). But as an integral part of that process, you really should be thinking of ways to improve it. So next time something bothers you about it, speak up. Your Team Lead can't read minds, and they really *need* to be aware of any issues you're facing.

Keep in mind, however, that it may even be your own habits that hold you back: e.g., you might be inclined to reinvent the wheel for every task. Or to pull in tons of dependencies for small things. Perhaps you write code that is too specific. Or, and this is a scenario I've seen quite often, your code is far too general and abstracted, while the problem at hand is the exact opposite.

Learning what the best approach is takes time and patience. But the good news is, there is a simple way to expedite that process: i.e., asking people with more experience and listening to what they have to say. One of the best habits to develop is to *seek meaningful feedback*. And to do so as often as possible.

# Teamwork Is Key

One of the truths we all need to understand and internalise is, the apparent dichotomy Engineer-Manager is fundamentally flawed. The best managers are the people who have *led or are leading* teams, and that means they must make certain everyone understands that we are collectively responsible for the software we are creating – in every sense of the word.

It's up to us, as a team, to enforce best practices, to choose the best tools for the job, and to deal with the inexorably growing complexity of non-trivial solutions. Only together can we find the best path forward and create true, lasting value – and as a leader, a vital part of your role is to convince your team of that each and every day.

# Chapter 17: Unwavering Discipline

## Constraints as Freedom

One of the 'secrets' I discovered early on in my career was that the best performing engineers were those with the most solid work ethic – the ones who, even when the going got really tough, remained calm, focused, and professional. They never complained and always had the right attitude towards the situation – however difficult it may be. They're the people who come into the office, get right to work, and get more done by noon than most people achieve throughout the entire day.

## The Path to Freedom

Discipline and focus are the main ingredients for success in just about any human endeavour. But especially in our industry, your ability to maintain both will set you apart from the majority. It will ensure you go the extra mile when you simply *must*. And it will – eventually – make you free.

What I mean by that is, the more time you spend at work actually *working*, the more you will achieve (no surprise there) – and usually do it in less time than people who waste their hours in the office. What's stopping you, at that point, from leaving early and working on a side hustle – or simply enjoying the rest of your day? So take a moment to consider the following: we are part of a very results-oriented industry, and achieving those results more quickly will, in the long run, bring you either more promotions or more free time – or, ideally, both.

Most important of all, be consistent. Never let past successes make you overconfident. Every new day and problem, and situation is a test of our will and resolve. And it's easier to fail than you think.

# The Cost of Performance

Everything said so far is also true for teams – with the added challenge, however, that multiple standards of excellence usually exist when we bring two or more engineers together. It's extremely difficult to achieve alignment of the expectations of individual team members, and it's a challenge for both the engineers and the leader.

But adding constraints, setting ground rules, relying on coding styles, patterns, conventions, and standard procedures – all of that removes friction and enables a team to perform at previously unattainable, even unimaginable, levels. It has an upfront cost in terms of the time spent setting them up and most likely the egos bruised when quality and performance discussions with team members occur (it's unpleasant on both sides of the conversation, I know). Is it a cost most teams should pay, however?

Opinions, as usual, lie scattered across the entire spectrum – yet, I am a strong proponent of making that investment at the earliest possible stage of a project. Have the difficult conversations, make the tough choices, and stand by your decisions.

The good thing is, all this may be initiated by any team member, so if you see an opportunity for improvement in your current team setup, or process, or coding practices, even if you're not the official leader, go for it. You might be surprised how well it will be accepted and how much it will pay off in the long run.

## Now We Are Free

All the effort and pain, the intense focus and the long hours – these are all worth it to build an amazing team. A single engineer, no matter how brilliant, will always be outshone by an organised and dedicated group of good devs focused on a unified goal.

> *'You are the best; the elite.'* [10] —*Obi-Wan Kenobi*

Ultimately, only coherent, disciplined, consistent teams blaze a shining path through the darkness of mediocrity. Striving to be better and better, seeking excellence in everything you collectively do, not only earns you the respect of others, but ensures their lasting trust in your abilities. And best of all – it wins you the freedom to one day set the direction yourself.

# Chapter 18: The Nature of Responsibility and Leadership

## Burden and Honour

In my experience, the vast majority of newly-minted leaders will fall into two broad categories: the Confident and the Worriers. If you're anything like me, you will start out in the second group. But fret not, for there is a way out and to greater things. Let me elaborate on that for a bit.

There are some people, to whom leadership is as easy as breathing. They seem to instinctively know what to say, how to react, the precise amount of work they need to do and/or delegate, which task should have the highest priority, and how to keep everyone from losing their minds during a crisis.

When I first dabbled in technical leadership, I most certainly did *not* belong to the group described above. On the contrary, I was very often at a loss for words, sometimes reacted more emotionally than rationally, took on too much work for my own good, had little clue what direction a project should go in, and my anxiety compounded tense situations and made them that much more problematic. And perhaps worst of all, I worried about making even the smallest decision for fear it would make someone angry – or that it would simply be wrong, I would fail spectacularly, and it would cost everyone time and money.

*'The greatest teacher, failure is.'* [11] –
*Yoda*

The oh-so-obvious secret is, you *can* move from one group to the other – though becoming confident is significantly harder than starting to worry a bit too much. And what Master Yoda told Luke is, in my opinion, the only way to ensure that outcome. What you need to do is to accept that Failure will be your constant companion and learn as much as possible from even the tiniest of mistakes. This acceptance will embolden you: in time, you will start making better and better choices and become better equipped to handle any challenge your job might throw at you.

But the even greater secret, the secret of both groups, is that they *do the work* – whatever the outward appearance, they do the work required to make things flow smoothly, keep the team happy and productive, keep the client satisfied with the money-to-value ratio, and keep their own leaders certain that they have placed their trust in the right person.

## The Worriers

Mistakes are just another way to grow as a leader, as I mentioned above. And one of the worst mistakes I made when I was just starting out was to take on all the work for myself. This one was very painful, and it took me a while to recognise it for what it was.

What's wrong with that, you might ask? So did I.

Isn't a technical leader supposed to be good at writing code – even the best one in the team at doing that? That's what I thought, too.

The truth is, this approach is misguided on a number of levels and usually stems from fear and arrogance: thinking no one else on your team can do the work as well as you is not only (usually) wrong, it's also a priority ticket to Arrogant Asshole town (see Chapter 5). Furthermore, the more you do that, the more stressed and overworked you become. Mistakes accumulate. You reach a boiling point and Failure is joined by Burnout. And the funny thing is, this tyrannical style – this strong desire for control – actually makes you weaker as a leader. The sooner you recognise and accept that, the sooner you can start moving to the other side of the spectrum.

## The Confident

The more you grow as a leader, the more you realise that you can get more done with a laid-back, *laissez faire* approach – within reason, of course. And *you* must choose where the line is drawn.

In my experience, there are a few things you *must* do:

1.  Be the most amazing professional you can be and constantly work on improving every aspect of yourself.

2. Learn to trust your team and delegate as much as you can – especially tasks that are challenging, interesting, and likely to help them grow as engineers (but never at the expense of the project and the client); and you should be *jubilant*, if someone on the team is better at coding than you are: rather than think of them as competition, you should learn how to leverage that skill and achieve greater results as a team.

3. Do the *actual* work, because your personal example is a shining beacon for your team, whether you realise it or not; in an industry as practical as ours, your authority stems from being deeply technical, while doing the rest of the non-technical work engineers often don't *want* to do.

There are, undoubtedly, many other aspects of leadership we can delve into, as well as many more I am yet to discover and internalise myself. Yet, if you find that some or all of these don't describe you at least partially, you should pause for a second and consider, if you're doing your absolute best – for yourself, your team, and your company.

## Why Lead?

It's at this point that some of you might begin to wonder, why do all this? What's the point of taking on all this additional responsibility – usually for a less-than-glamorous pay raise?

For better or worse, I have no clear-cut answer for this one. Personally, I've always been fascinated by both 'worlds' – i.e., creating software and leading the teams doing that. Saying that it's a calling may be a bit too much, but that's how I've chosen to interpret it.

Responsibility is the ultimate honour, as well as the heaviest burden. When you get to a certain level and the fate of the project rests on your shoulders, and so does the success of the team… things are not as black-and-white as when you're just writing code. But once you choose to accept that responsibility, to take ownership of everything about it, you rise to a new level and become a true leader.

It's not easy. It shouldn't be. But it's worth it.

# Chapter 19: A Brief Treatise on the Toxicity of Culture

## Why Context Matters

In my experience, there are few concepts more over-hyped and misunderstood than what we collectively define as Company Culture.

Not only are the details of that idea entirely shaped by subjective interpretation, but we all have different preferences for – and are comfortable in – discrete environments. Some may thrive in a fast-paced start-up, while others prefer the more established processes in a larger, more mature company.

Whatever your interpretation might be, you have probably already encountered a culture that you would define as 'toxic' – to yourself, at the very least. And although the notions delineated in this chapter so far are a bit too ephemeral for my liking, there are *some* common markers of a terrible company culture that we could all agree on.

## Define Healthy

My upside-down approach to the definition of 'toxic' begins with a few words on what a 'healthy' culture might look like in the Software Engineering world (and beyond).

There are numerous large and small details that fit my definition. Here are several aspects of a good company culture I have come across over the years:

1.  You are encouraged to become better as a person and an engineer. Or in more concrete terms, your employer does *not* neglect your growth. This usually entails a clear path to the Senior Engineer title (and beyond), as well as transparency regarding the criteria for achieving that: to be more specific, you must, at all times, know what skills you need to work on in order to level up. It also means that you

are likely to get frequent one-on-one meetings with your manager about your career goals – a syncing of Interpretations of the Future, if you will. That's doubly true *after* you become someone's manager: not only should your boss take the time to sync, but so should you – with each and every member of your team. And most important of all, feedback should flow both ways.

2. The office is permeated by a willingness to work together towards a common goal. Everyone understands that they must solve problems as a team (as we discussed in Chapter 16), or they *will* fail as individuals. This is perhaps too obvious to even mention, but it is so fundamental that I *cannot* omit it.

3. No one is counting the minutes of work, because nothing ensures burnout more completely than a micromanaging tyrant tracking every minute of an engineer's time. And good managers know that neither lines of code, nor hours sitting in your chair will define how valuable your contributions are to the company. In places where people know that, you can have a semblance of balance between work and life, because staying late at the office is *not* the only way to get a promotion.

4. A good culture is also defined by the attitude towards failure. I've noticed that it is

commonly framed as a learning opportunity, rather than the end of the bloody world. Briefly put, being afraid of making the tiniest mistake because it might cost you your job is not the best motivator when it comes to growing as an engineer. Of course, the sheer stupidity and grandeur of the mistake should be kept in mind – there is a sizable gap between the occasional small slip-up and repeatedly making a complete mess due to utter incompetence. To put that in more concrete terms, think of it as the difference between missing one edge case in your implementation and dropping all the tables from the production database.

5. It goes without saying, but bears repeating nonetheless: no racism and no sexism (a.k.a., Being a Professional and a Decent Human Being 101). Measure yourself and others by the excellence of your work – or lack thereof. Which is not to say that a good company culture is based on *judgement*. Quite the contrary, in fact: this is obvious and very much related to the previous point on failure, but a culture of public blaming and shaming is incredibly detrimental to *any* team in *any* industry. Good teams don't play the blame game – they learn from their mistakes and move on.

## High Levels of Toxicity

I would define a toxic culture as the antithesis of the far-from-exhaustive list we just went through: if you feel stuck in your career or isolated in your efforts, or constantly prodded to work harder, you most certainly are *not* in a good place work-wise. If you dread making even the simplest of mistakes or are constantly blamed and judged by others, you are definitely dealing with a toxic culture.

> '*Why should a man be scorned if,*
> *finding himself in prison, he tries to*
> *get out and go home?*' [12] — *J.R.R.*
> *Tolkien*

In the vast majority of cases, if you find yourself in a place like that, in the metaphorical prison of a horrible job, I believe you must do your utmost to move to a better one. Not all such cultures are beyond redemption, but are you really willing to pour your heart and soul into saving this one? And while I would never say that you should get up immediately and hand in your resignation (that would just be poor planning on your part), I do think that, ultimately, it is your only recourse.

It's somewhat more complicated when you're the leader, when you feel like you can make things better for your team and project, and department. But it's not categorically different: reshaping a culture is extremely hard and thankless work. And the results are rarely guaranteed, no matter your position in the pecking order. What's more or less guaranteed, however, is a general feeling of helplessness and despair.

So in the simplest of terms, I still think you have an obligation to yourself to seek work where you are valued and what you do has meaning – or at the very least, a place where you are not utterly miserable.

The truth is, there will always be companies with toxic cultures. But *we* make the choice to continue working for them. And we *can* make a better one.

# Chapter 20: Achievement Unlocked?

## Sacrifice and Success in the Software Engineering World

In Software Engineering, as in many other career paths, it can be disparagingly easy to lose sight of what truly matters: 'life, the universe, and everything' [13]. In the wonderful books by the amazing Douglas Adams, we never quite found out what the answer to that was. But we *do* know that we all seek it.

All jokes aside, however, our field *does* often demand extreme focus, and the work we do *can* become the centrepiece of our existence without us even realising it. But I guess the secret to not letting that happen – if indeed one wants to avoid it – is quite simple: you should simply think of work in terms of how it will make your life much better, not as your entire life.

However, that certainly is more easily said than done. Indeed, it can be among the most difficult habits and modes of thinking to develop, especially if you want an amazing career as a Software Engineer. Still, one must always ask themselves, does any of it matter? Why am I doing this? Especially if they're miserable every day of their life (see the previous chapter).

A relatively healthy perspective is the perception of a career as a marathon, rather than a sprint. What I mean by that is, it's completely fine to want to become great and work towards it, but it's healthy to take your foot off the gas pedal once in a while – at least a little bit. Because blowing your engine, if I may extend the car metaphor, will never get you as far on that road trip as easing off the throttle, taking your time, and opting for the scenic route.

After all, one should try to enjoy the long and winding path to success, even if they never quite get there. And it shouldn't be to the detriment of all other aspects of their life (as we already established above). Also, burnout is never fun – trust me, I know.

And on that note, it pays off to learn to set the right goals: to think about where said journey might lead you and choose the best way to get to that place. But, and I'll say it again, take your time. The most amazing results are often attained one small step at a time. No one has ever become a Senior Engineer in a day (as far as I'm aware, that is).

It may take years and years of hard work – but that work must be offset by *something*. Being on the treadmill non-stop can only ever ensure an irreversible descent into madness. And the truth is, sometimes you need time off to *become better at your job*.

When you're constantly too deep in the code or too close to a project, you can't see the bigger picture. Getting a bit of distance grants clarity and perspective and increases the likelihood of randomly-occurring 'Eureka!' moments. I just love it when some complex issue I couldn't resolve after days of work suddenly becomes very clear as I'm walking through the park on a day off and quite pointedly *not* thinking about it.

A few things you *should* be thinking about more often, however, are your fears and insecurities. Being honest with yourself regarding those is a difficult first step towards *not* letting them dictate your decisions – especially if you're leading a team and every single decision matters. I would summarise this point as follows: never cling to a job or a project, or a technology. In the words of the great Master Yoda, 'Train yourself to let go of everything you fear to lose.' [14] Accepting that everything is transient, if I may interpret these words in such a way, will make you stronger and more resolute. And you will then have the courage to stand against the myriad ways a project and a team can become royally… *wrong*.

Rather than betting on the safe option, you should try to forge your own path, to find your place in the world, to climb the particular heights of success that inspire and motivate *you*.

Because a job *should not* make you miserable, but neither is it supposed to make you happy (though it's obviously fine, if it does). It's better, I believe, to strive to find work and to do work which is fulfilling and meaningful – at least to you and those around you.

Indeed, we have no choice but to try to do what builds us up and makes us want to be better tomorrow than we are today, makes us *dream* of being so much more. For how else can we become?

# Epilogue: Sine Qua Non

## What makes a leader worthy of the title?

Before you read further, I'd like to take the opportunity to thank you for making it this far: to the end of my relatively short book about the long and arduous journey to the mantle of technical leadership. Its brevity notwithstanding, I hope you have found valuable information and important lessons within these pages – or at the very least, some food for thought.

I've been talking about leadership in the last circa twenty chapters, but I never once stopped to ask the question, what makes a leader worthy of the name? What's the main prerequisite – if indeed we can actually define one? And to be perfectly honest, I have no clear and simple answer, if only for the simple reason that I'm constantly discovering new depths and uncovering new mysteries – and so will you, one day.

*'Those things we deem essential,*
*without which we cannot bear living.*
*Without which life in general loses its*
*specific value, becomes abstract.'* [15] –
Romo Lampkin

What I *can* say with some degree of certainty, however, is that there are some indubitable, inextricable, inexorable requirements. There are certain qualities that I would dub the *sine qua non* of being a leader – and please interpret this not in the legal sense, but rather as a metaphor: i.e., more along the lines it was used in the 2004 *Battlestar Galactica* reboot. Counsellor Lampkin and Admiral Adama had one of the saddest and most poignant conversations in the entire series. If you haven't seen it, you most definitely *should*.

But I digress. The question is, what is it that deprives a leader of the meaning inherent in the title? And contrary-wise, which qualities flesh out the title, lest it become just an empty word?

In my experience, a leader is a person who:

1. Knows when to follow, yet also knows when to step up and lead; when to listen and when to speak.
2. Takes ownership of failure, but shares the credit for success.
3. Always fights for what they know is right, even when the price seems too high.

4. Understands that leadership is *service*: you serve the goals of each and every member of your team, as well as those of your superiors and your clients – you *never* come first.

5. Helps his peers grow as professionals and is constantly thinking of ways to inspire and motivate them.

6. Knows when to shield their team, and knows when to put them in the 'line of fire'.

7. Seeks to make a positive impact and create lasting value, rather than climb a career ladder and get a quick pay raise.

8. Stands by their words and lets honesty and transparency dictate them, rather than twist them to serve some ulterior motive.

The collection of qualities and behavioural patterns goes on and on – or at least they do in my head. And while it will never be exhaustive, I will top it off with the following: above all else, I believe a leader is a real person, a well-rounded human being with emotions, and hobbies, and interests, and duties *beyond the office*. A person who is not afraid to state that life is more than work – and is accepting both of themselves and of their team.

Aspirational though this list may be, I do believe in each and every item on it, and I *know* that you will be a better leader, if you follow at least some of them. The path is long and difficult, but you *will* make it to the end – and beyond.

# Sources

1. Star Wars: Episode V – The Empire Strikes Back (1980)
2. Star Wars: Episode I – The Phantom Menace (1999)
3. Star Wars: Episode II – Attack of the Clones (2002)
4. On Writing: A Memoir of the Craft (2000), Stephen King
5. Star Wars: Episode II – Attack of the Clones (2002)
6. Star Wars: The Clone Wars (2008)
7. Star Wars Republic Commando: Order 66 (2008), Karen Traviss
8. Star Wars Rebels, Season 3, Episode 20, Twin Suns (2017)
9. The Bromeliad Trilogy: Diggers (1990), Terry Pratchett
10. Star Wars: Clone Wars, Chapter 2 (2003)
11. Star Wars: Episode VIII – The Last Jedi (2017)
12. Tolkien on Fairy-stories (2008), J.R.R. Tolkien, Verlyn Flieger (Editor), Douglas A. Anderson (Editor)
13. The Hitchhiker's Guide to the Galaxy (1979), Douglas Adams
14. Star Wars: Episode III - Revenge of the Sith (2005)

# About the Author

A tinkerer by heart, he believes one should always leave the code better than they found it - and apply the same to everything.

You can learn more about him at https://bozhinov.me/.